Race Against Time

Shahanara Alam

Race Against Time by Shahanara Alam

Copyright © 2023 Shahanara Alam

First edition 2023

…To my loving husband
and my lovely children…

…A special thank you to
everyone I love and care,
some of them do and others
don't know who they are…

…To my loving husband
and my lovely children…

…A special thank you to
everyone I love and care,
some of them do and others
don't know who they are…

Contents

True Love

True love is not easy to find,
I am looking for it,
looking for it,
in my crazy mind.
I have found it,
found it in my heart,
please my Lord,
do not let it depart.
Absence of true love,
is a barrier,
presence of true love,
lets me go higher.
I believe, true love,
only comes from You
and lasts beyond reality,
O my Lord,
let us be in love for eternity.

Thanks

Wish to say thank you,
Thank you for being with me,
I am so grateful to you,
oh my family.
The illness makes my life unbearable,
that is the feeling it gives me,
thank you for being so understanding,
oh my family.
Surviving becomes hard
and eases slowly,
thank you for being so strong,
oh my family.
Your love makes me a survivor,
that's the feeling constantly,
thank you for being so caring,
oh my family.
I am praying for your success of
Deen and Duniya,
oh my loving family,
please my Lord,
accept my prayer and
forgive everyone including me.

Glowing Path

Show us the way,
show us the way,
let the path glow,
please my Lord,
do not say no.
I am searching for the path,
path in my mind,
Please my Lord,
make it easy,
as You are so kind.
Only You can show the way,
sorry my Lord,
we are unable,
unable to pay.
I believe, Your guidance,
is the glowing path,
path to success
of Deen and Duniya,
please my Lord,
let us find the way,
long before we leave
for Akhirah.

My Mother

Cannot bear the absence,
absence of my mother,
the pain is terrible,
even the thought is a killer.
Have to say goodbye,
goodbye to my mother,
we are not here to stay,
cannot stay forever.
Want to make the most of my mother,
in Duniya,
please my Lord,
accept my effort,
before her transfer.
Your kindness,
is what I am after,
please my Lord,
be kind to my mother.

Human Nature

I wish to be perfect,
perfect, I cannot be,
no one is perfect,
that is what I see.
I wish we were angels,
angels, we cannot be,
everyone makes mistakes,
that is what I see.
I wish we were faultless,
faultless, we cannot be,
we are a mixture
of good and bad,
that is what I see.
I wish we had patience,
patient, we cannot be,
it is human nature,
that is what I see.

Pure Love

It is sweet,
sweet to share a heart,
pure love,
pure love is playing a part.
This is the love,
I was in search for,
please my Lord,
accept my thanks
and bless us more.
You are so kind and clever,
O my Lord,
increase our love,
for each-other.
I believe, it is coming,
coming from You,
love is my strength,
that is my view.
I didn't realise the importance,
importance of love, in this life,
please my Lord,
let it remain, also in the after-life.

My Baby

I didn't give birth to her,
she is my baby.
I didn't have sleepless nights,
because of her,
she is my baby.
I didn't change her nappy,
didn't feed her,
she is my baby.
I didn't change her clothes,
didn't bathe her,
she is my baby.
I didn't hear her cry,
didn't hug her,
she is my baby.
I didn't see her first smile,
didn't kiss her,
she is my baby...
It's a pleasure to have her,
she is my baby.
Please my Lord,
take care of my baby.

My Parents

They are the reason
for me to be here today,
I am in debt to them,
unable to pay.
Their memory will remain
even if they leave,
I'll cherish their love
as long as I live.
They are in my thought
and in my heart,
it's a blessing to have them
even if they depart.
Wish I knew more
beautiful words to say,
all I can do is pray.
Praying for their comfort
in Duniya and in Akhirah,
please my Lord,
keep my parents in pleasures
of the highest Jannah.

Crave

I am afraid,
afraid of the grave,
pleasures of Jannah,
is my crave.
I am afraid of the darkness,
darkness in the grave,
pleasures of Jannah,
is my crave.
I am afraid of the tightness,
tightness in the grave,
pleasures of Jannah,
is my crave.
I am afraid of the questions,
questions in the grave,
pleasures of Jannah,
is my crave.
I am afraid of Your fury,
afraid of your fury constantly,
please my Lord,
let me indulge
in pleasures of Jannah, thankfully.

Carefree Life

Roses are beautiful,
beautiful blue sky,
it's a wonderful feeling
to see a cute butterfly.
Birds are singing,
singing nearby,
pigeons have come to my view
and off they fly.
They are flying,
flying not so far,
wish to be carefree,
carefree as they are.
Seeing them in my garden,
over and over again,
enjoying the pleasure
also in the rain.
The rain has stopped,
it's a beautiful summer day,
gazing at nature,
takes my breath away.

My Gems

Oh my children,
I love you, I love you, I love you.
You are the pieces of my heart,
living is hard by being apart.
You are my survival kit,
you are my special treat.
You are my treasure
and my pleasure.
Your love pulls me up from the grave,
Your happiness is my crave.
You are my spring
and my Lord's blessing.
Life is lifeless, without you,
oh my gems,
I love you, I love you, I love you.

Hidden Future

Future is which,
I am searching to see,
wish I knew,
what does it hold for me.
Future is which,
impossible to see,
as my vision is blurry,
blurry vision clearly.
Future is which,
not easy to see,
it is unknown,
unknown it will be.
Future is which,
not for me to see,
it will remain unseen,
unseen and hidden from me.

Race Against Time

I am racing,
racing towards the grave,
even though, living is my crave.
Fifty years of my life
has left me,
I am not here for eternity.
Time is running fast,
my existence will not last.
I am only a traveller,
not here forever.
The journey is ending,
I think I am leaving.
Leaving for good,
this is the thought
of my low mood.

Sweet Sixteen

Wanted to be a writer,
long time ago,
head became blank,
mind said no.
I was thirsty,
thirsty for writing,
couldn't think,
think of anything.
I began after a very long time,
felt like, my Lord was
holding the pen
and teaching me,
how to rhyme.
Started writing,
in March twenty fifteen,
even though, my desire
was to write,
when I was, sweet sixteen.

The Gift

I have received my gift,
gift I was longing to see,
It is so precious,
precious to me.
It's a cure
for my low mood,
gives me endless pleasure,
makes me feel good.
It is a therapy
for my fragile mind,
priceless it is,
it is one of a kind.
Many, many thanks
for the special gift,
please my Lord,
accept my thanks and
don't let me drift.

Rusty Heart

I am nothing without You,
please my Lord,
erase every sin,
old and new.
My mind is a blend
of good and bad,
please my Lord,
give me a clean head.
I am dirty and have a
rusty body-part,
please my Lord,
give me a pure heart.
Pure heart and a clean head,
that is what I need,
please my Lord,
accept our every good deed.
In return,
I want a treasure,
please my Lord,
bless me with Your pleasure.

Wedding Gift

It's the beginning of
your new life together,
your Lord is your guide,
always remember.
Be nice and kind
to each other,
keep your hearts full of love,
never make it empty, never.
Thank your Lord,
every moment, everyday,
Thank Him,
Thank Him, especially today.
Your Lord will help you,
overcome every difficulty,
call Him all the time,
call Him sincerely.
Wish to see you smiling
and being happy,
wish you all the best
for your new life journey.

Beauty of Dawn

Wow!
It's a beautiful sky,
never seen this beauty,
I wonder, why?
The pattern is amazing,
superb is the colour,
I think the sky went to
a beauty parlour.
The beautician is a great artist,
that is my view,
I know it's You my Lord,
I know it's You.
Stunning beauty of dawn,
has caught my eyes today,
I am breathless,
what else can I say?

Long-Lost Treasure

Lost my children,
lost them for good,
that is the thought I had,
during the start of my low mood.
They were in my heart,
in my heart only,
missed their presence,
missed them dearly.
Lost them for,
two and a half years exactly,
I was with them yet,
they were far away from me.
My Lord gave them back to me,
in February,
two thousand and three.
Wish to thank Him
For giving me such pleasure,
as they are the gems of my eyes
and my long-lost treasure.

Thirst

I need to learn,
learning is what I need,
being taught by the best teacher,
best teacher indeed.
He is an amazing tutor,
tutoring through life,
He will teach me,
till it's time for the afterlife.
He is so generous
and very nice to me,
all He wants,
is to love Him dearly.
You are my Master,
Master in my heart,
quench my thirst my Lord,
quench my thirst.